50 French Shake Recipes for Home

By: Kelly Johnson

Table of Contents

- Café au Lait Shake
- Crème Brûlée Shake
- Madeleine Shake
- Raspberry Macaron Shake
- Tarte Tatin Shake
- Lemon Curd Shake
- Parisian Chocolate Shake
- Eclair Shake
- Chocolat Chaud Shake
- Vanilla Panna Cotta Shake
- Pistachio Éclair Shake
- Crêpe Suzette Shake
- French Toast Shake
- Mango Madeleine Shake
- Chocolat Praliné Shake
- Raspberry Sorbet Shake
- Peach Clafoutis Shake
- Almond Croissant Shake
- Lemon Meringue Shake
- Brioche and Jam Shake
- Profiterole Shake
- Nutella Crêpe Shake
- Lavender Honey Shake
- Cassis Shake
- Apple Tartelette Shake
- Café au Lait Crème Shake
- Gingerbread Macaron Shake
- Chardonnay Peach Shake
- Vanilla Bean Crêpe Shake
- Berry Compote Shake
- Chocolate Hazelnut Croissant Shake
- Lemon Basil Shake

- Raspberry Ganache Shake
- Honey Almond Shake
- Pear Clafoutis Shake
- Orange Blossom Shake
- Banana Chocolate Croissant Shake
- Crème Fraîche Shake
- Strawberry Mille-Feuille Shake
- Bordeaux Wine Shake
- Creme Caramel Shake
- Fig and Honey Shake
- Blueberry Lavender Shake
- Vacherin Shake
- Choco-Mint Macaron Shake
- Blackberry Tart Shake
- Almond Cream Shake
- Raspberry Chiffon Shake
- Caramelized Banana Shake
- Brioche Bread Pudding Shake

Café au Lait Shake

Ingredients:

- 1 cup milk (dairy or non-dairy, such as almond or oat milk)
- 1/2 cup vanilla ice cream (or dairy-free vanilla ice cream)
- 1/2 cup brewed coffee (cooled; strong coffee or espresso is best)
- 1/4 cup Greek yogurt (plain or vanilla)
- 1 tablespoon sugar or sweetener (optional, to taste)
- 1/4 teaspoon vanilla extract
- Ice cubes (as needed)
- Optional: Whipped cream and a sprinkle of cocoa powder or cinnamon (for garnish)

Instructions:

1. **Prepare Coffee:**
    - Brew your coffee or espresso and let it cool to room temperature. For a stronger flavor, use espresso or a strong coffee blend.
2. **Blend Ingredients:**
    - In a blender, combine the milk, vanilla ice cream, cooled coffee, Greek yogurt, sugar (if using), and vanilla extract.
3. **Add Ice:**
    - Add a handful of ice cubes for a thicker, colder shake.
4. **Blend:**
    - Blend on high until smooth and creamy. If the shake is too thick, add more milk to reach your desired consistency.
5. **Taste and Adjust:**
    - Taste the shake and adjust sweetness if needed by adding more sugar or sweetener.
6. **Serve:**
    - Pour the shake into a glass. Optionally, top with whipped cream and a sprinkle of cocoa powder or cinnamon for a decorative touch.

Enjoy your Café au Lait Shake! It's a creamy and indulgent treat that brings the classic flavors of a French café au lait into a refreshing milkshake.

Crème Brûlée Shake

Ingredients:

- 1 cup milk (dairy or non-dairy, such as almond or oat milk)
- 1/2 cup vanilla ice cream (or dairy-free vanilla ice cream)
- 1/2 cup heavy cream
- 1/4 cup crème brûlée or vanilla custard (store-bought or homemade)
- 1 tablespoon brown sugar (for caramelizing)
- 1/4 teaspoon vanilla extract
- Ice cubes (as needed)
- Optional: Whipped cream and additional brown sugar for garnish

Instructions:

1. **Prepare Crème Brûlée/Custard:**
    - If using store-bought crème brûlée or custard, ensure it is chilled before using. If making homemade custard, allow it to cool completely before using.
2. **Blend Ingredients:**
    - In a blender, combine the milk, vanilla ice cream, heavy cream, crème brûlée or custard, and vanilla extract.
3. **Add Ice:**
    - Add a handful of ice cubes for a thicker, colder shake.
4. **Blend:**
    - Blend on high until smooth and creamy. If the shake is too thick, add more milk to achieve your desired consistency.
5. **Taste and Adjust:**
    - Taste the shake and adjust sweetness if needed. You can add a little more custard or a splash of vanilla extract if desired.
6. **Caramelize Brown Sugar:**
    - For a caramelized sugar effect, sprinkle a thin layer of brown sugar on top of the shake and use a kitchen torch to caramelize it. If you don't have a torch, you can omit this step or use pre-made caramel sauce for a similar effect.
7. **Serve:**
    - Pour the shake into a glass. Optionally, top with whipped cream and an extra sprinkle of brown sugar for garnish.

Enjoy your Crème Brûlée Shake! It's a creamy and indulgent treat that brings the luxurious flavors of crème brûlée into a refreshing milkshake.

Madeleine Shake

Ingredients:

- 1 cup milk (dairy or non-dairy, such as almond or oat milk)
- 1/2 cup vanilla ice cream (or dairy-free vanilla ice cream)
- 1/2 cup Greek yogurt (plain or vanilla)
- 4-6 madeleine cookies (store-bought or homemade)
- 1 tablespoon honey or maple syrup (optional, for extra sweetness)
- 1/4 teaspoon vanilla extract
- Zest of 1 lemon
- Ice cubes (as needed)
- Optional: Whipped cream and additional madeleine cookie crumbs for garnish

Instructions:

1. **Prepare Madeleine Cookies:**
   - If using homemade or store-bought madeleine cookies, crumble them into small pieces. You can lightly toast them if desired for extra flavor.
2. **Blend Ingredients:**
   - In a blender, combine the milk, vanilla ice cream, Greek yogurt, crumbled madeleine cookies, honey or maple syrup (if using), vanilla extract, and lemon zest.
3. **Add Ice:**
   - Add a handful of ice cubes for a thicker, colder shake.
4. **Blend:**
   - Blend on high until smooth and creamy. If the shake is too thick, add more milk to reach your desired consistency.
5. **Taste and Adjust:**
   - Taste the shake and adjust sweetness or lemon flavor if needed by adding more honey or lemon zest.
6. **Serve:**
   - Pour the shake into a glass. Optionally, top with whipped cream and a sprinkle of additional madeleine cookie crumbs for a decorative touch.

Enjoy your Madeleine Shake! It's a creamy, flavorful treat that brings the classic taste of French madeleine cookies into a refreshing and indulgent milkshake.

Raspberry Macaron Shake

Ingredients:

- 1 cup milk (dairy or non-dairy, such as almond or oat milk)
- 1/2 cup vanilla ice cream (or dairy-free vanilla ice cream)
- 1/2 cup Greek yogurt (plain or vanilla)
- 1/2 cup fresh or frozen raspberries
- 2-3 raspberry macarons (store-bought or homemade, crumbled)
- 1 tablespoon honey or maple syrup (optional, for extra sweetness)
- 1/4 teaspoon vanilla extract
- Ice cubes (as needed)
- Optional: Whipped cream and extra crumbled macarons for garnish

Instructions:

1. **Prepare Raspberries:**
   - If using fresh raspberries, wash them. If using frozen, let them thaw slightly before using.
2. **Prepare Macarons:**
   - If using store-bought or homemade raspberry macarons, crumble them into small pieces.
3. **Blend Ingredients:**
   - In a blender, combine the milk, vanilla ice cream, Greek yogurt, raspberries, crumbled macarons, honey or maple syrup (if using), and vanilla extract.
4. **Add Ice:**
   - Add a handful of ice cubes for a thicker, colder shake.
5. **Blend:**
   - Blend on high until smooth and creamy. If the shake is too thick, add more milk to achieve your desired consistency.
6. **Taste and Adjust:**
   - Taste the shake and adjust sweetness or raspberry flavor if needed by adding more honey or additional raspberries.
7. **Serve:**
   - Pour the shake into a glass. Optionally, top with whipped cream and a sprinkle of extra crumbled macarons for a decorative and indulgent touch.

Enjoy your Raspberry Macaron Shake! It's a creamy and fruity treat that captures the elegant flavors of French raspberry macarons in a refreshing milkshake.

Tarte Tatin Shake

Ingredients:

- 1 cup milk (dairy or non-dairy, such as almond or oat milk)
- 1/2 cup vanilla ice cream (or dairy-free vanilla ice cream)
- 1/2 cup Greek yogurt (plain or vanilla)
- 1 cup apple slices (peeled and cored; fresh or frozen)
- 2 tablespoons caramel sauce (store-bought or homemade)
- 1 tablespoon brown sugar (optional, for extra caramel flavor)
- 1/4 teaspoon cinnamon
- 1/4 teaspoon vanilla extract
- Ice cubes (as needed)
- Optional: Whipped cream and extra caramel sauce for garnish

Instructions:

1. **Prepare Apples:**
    - If using fresh apples, peel, core, and slice them. You can lightly sauté the apple slices in a pan with a bit of butter and a sprinkle of brown sugar and cinnamon to enhance the caramelized flavor. Allow them to cool before using. If using frozen apples, let them thaw slightly.
2. **Blend Ingredients:**
    - In a blender, combine the milk, vanilla ice cream, Greek yogurt, apple slices, caramel sauce, brown sugar (if using), cinnamon, and vanilla extract.
3. **Add Ice:**
    - Add a handful of ice cubes for a thicker, colder shake.
4. **Blend:**
    - Blend on high until smooth and creamy. If the shake is too thick, add more milk to achieve your desired consistency.
5. **Taste and Adjust:**
    - Taste the shake and adjust sweetness or caramel flavor if needed by adding more caramel sauce or brown sugar.
6. **Serve:**
    - Pour the shake into a glass. Optionally, top with whipped cream and a drizzle of extra caramel sauce for a decorative and indulgent touch.

Enjoy your Tarte Tatin Shake! It's a creamy, flavorful treat that brings the rich, caramelized flavors of the classic French dessert into a refreshing milkshake.

Lemon Curd Shake

Ingredients:

- 1 cup milk (dairy or non-dairy, such as almond or oat milk)
- 1/2 cup vanilla ice cream (or dairy-free vanilla ice cream)
- 1/2 cup Greek yogurt (plain or vanilla)
- 1/4 cup lemon curd (store-bought or homemade)
- 1 tablespoon honey or maple syrup (optional, for extra sweetness)
- 1/4 teaspoon vanilla extract
- Zest of 1 lemon
- Ice cubes (as needed)
- Optional: Whipped cream and extra lemon zest for garnish

Instructions:

1. **Prepare Lemon Curd:**
   - If using homemade lemon curd, ensure it is chilled before using. If using store-bought, give it a good stir before adding to the shake.
2. **Blend Ingredients:**
   - In a blender, combine the milk, vanilla ice cream, Greek yogurt, lemon curd, honey or maple syrup (if using), vanilla extract, and lemon zest.
3. **Add Ice:**
   - Add a handful of ice cubes for a thicker, colder shake.
4. **Blend:**
   - Blend on high until smooth and creamy. If the shake is too thick, add more milk to achieve your desired consistency.
5. **Taste and Adjust:**
   - Taste the shake and adjust sweetness or lemon flavor if needed by adding more honey or lemon curd.
6. **Serve:**
   - Pour the shake into a glass. Optionally, top with whipped cream and a sprinkle of extra lemon zest for a decorative and zesty touch.

Enjoy your Lemon Curd Shake! It's a creamy, tangy treat that brings the bright, citrusy flavors of lemon curd into a refreshing milkshake.

Parisian Chocolate Shake

Ingredients:

- 1 cup milk (dairy or non-dairy, such as almond or oat milk)
- 1/2 cup chocolate ice cream (or dairy-free chocolate ice cream)
- 1/4 cup Greek yogurt (plain or vanilla)
- 1/4 cup chocolate syrup (store-bought or homemade)
- 2 tablespoons brewed coffee (cooled; optional, for a mocha flavor)
- 1/4 teaspoon vanilla extract
- Ice cubes (as needed)
- Optional: Whipped cream, chocolate shavings, and a drizzle of chocolate syrup for garnish

Instructions:

1. **Prepare Coffee (Optional):**
   - Brew a small amount of coffee and let it cool. This step is optional but adds a mocha flavor to the shake.
2. **Blend Ingredients:**
   - In a blender, combine the milk, chocolate ice cream, Greek yogurt, chocolate syrup, brewed coffee (if using), and vanilla extract.
3. **Add Ice:**
   - Add a handful of ice cubes for a thicker, colder shake.
4. **Blend:**
   - Blend on high until smooth and creamy. If the shake is too thick, add more milk to achieve your desired consistency.
5. **Taste and Adjust:**
   - Taste the shake and adjust sweetness or chocolate flavor if needed by adding more chocolate syrup.
6. **Serve:**
   - Pour the shake into a glass. Optionally, top with whipped cream, a sprinkle of chocolate shavings, and a drizzle of chocolate syrup for a decadent touch.

Enjoy your Parisian Chocolate Shake! It's a rich and creamy treat that captures the elegance of Parisian chocolate desserts in a refreshing milkshake.

Eclair Shake

Ingredients:

- 1 cup milk (dairy or non-dairy, such as almond or oat milk)
- 1/2 cup vanilla ice cream (or dairy-free vanilla ice cream)
- 1/2 cup Greek yogurt (plain or vanilla)
- 4-6 éclairs (store-bought or homemade, crumbled)
- 2 tablespoons chocolate syrup (for the "glaze" effect)
- 1 tablespoon caramel sauce (optional, for extra sweetness)
- 1/4 teaspoon vanilla extract
- Ice cubes (as needed)
- Optional: Whipped cream, extra crumbled éclairs, and a drizzle of chocolate syrup for garnish

Instructions:

1. **Prepare Éclairs:**
    - If using store-bought or homemade éclairs, crumble them into small pieces. If desired, toast the crumbles lightly to enhance the flavor.
2. **Blend Ingredients:**
    - In a blender, combine the milk, vanilla ice cream, Greek yogurt, crumbled éclairs, chocolate syrup, caramel sauce (if using), and vanilla extract.
3. **Add Ice:**
    - Add a handful of ice cubes for a thicker, colder shake.
4. **Blend:**
    - Blend on high until smooth and creamy. If the shake is too thick, add more milk to achieve your desired consistency.
5. **Taste and Adjust:**
    - Taste the shake and adjust sweetness or flavor if needed by adding more chocolate syrup or caramel sauce.
6. **Serve:**
    - Pour the shake into a glass. Optionally, top with whipped cream, extra crumbled éclairs, and a drizzle of chocolate syrup for a decorative and indulgent touch.

Enjoy your Éclair Shake! It's a creamy and luxurious treat that brings the classic flavors of French éclairs into a refreshing milkshake.

Chocolat Chaud Shake

Ingredients:

- 1 cup milk (dairy or non-dairy, such as almond or oat milk)
- 1/2 cup chocolate ice cream (or dairy-free chocolate ice cream)
- 1/2 cup heavy cream
- 1/4 cup cocoa powder (unsweetened)
- 1/4 cup sugar (or to taste)
- 1/2 teaspoon vanilla extract
- 2 tablespoons chocolate syrup (optional, for extra chocolatey flavor)
- Ice cubes (as needed)
- Optional: Whipped cream, chocolate shavings, and a drizzle of chocolate syrup for garnish

Instructions:

1. **Prepare Chocolate Mixture:**
   - In a small saucepan, heat the milk over medium heat until warm but not boiling. Whisk in the cocoa powder and sugar until fully dissolved and combined. Remove from heat.
2. **Blend Ingredients:**
   - In a blender, combine the chocolate mixture, chocolate ice cream, heavy cream, and vanilla extract. Add the chocolate syrup if using.
3. **Add Ice:**
   - Add a handful of ice cubes for a thicker, colder shake.
4. **Blend:**
   - Blend on high until smooth and creamy. If the shake is too thick, add more milk to reach your desired consistency.
5. **Taste and Adjust:**
   - Taste the shake and adjust sweetness or chocolate flavor if needed by adding more sugar or chocolate syrup.
6. **Serve:**
   - Pour the shake into a glass. Optionally, top with whipped cream, chocolate shavings, and a drizzle of chocolate syrup for a decadent touch.

Enjoy your Chocolat Chaud Shake! It's a rich, creamy treat that brings the beloved flavors of French hot chocolate into a delightful milkshake.

Vanilla Panna Cotta Shake

Ingredients:

- 1 cup milk (dairy or non-dairy, such as almond or oat milk)
- 1/2 cup vanilla ice cream (or dairy-free vanilla ice cream)
- 1/2 cup heavy cream
- 1/4 cup vanilla panna cotta (store-bought or homemade)
- 1 tablespoon sugar or honey (optional, for extra sweetness)
- 1/4 teaspoon vanilla extract
- Ice cubes (as needed)
- Optional: Whipped cream and fresh berries for garnish

Instructions:

1. **Prepare Panna Cotta:**
   - If using store-bought panna cotta, make sure it is chilled. If making homemade panna cotta, ensure it has been allowed to set and is fully chilled before using.
2. **Blend Ingredients:**
   - In a blender, combine the milk, vanilla ice cream, heavy cream, vanilla panna cotta, and vanilla extract. If you want extra sweetness, add sugar or honey.
3. **Add Ice:**
   - Add a handful of ice cubes for a thicker, colder shake.
4. **Blend:**
   - Blend on high until smooth and creamy. If the shake is too thick, add more milk to achieve your desired consistency.
5. **Taste and Adjust:**
   - Taste the shake and adjust sweetness if needed by adding more sugar or honey.
6. **Serve:**
   - Pour the shake into a glass. Optionally, top with whipped cream and fresh berries for a touch of elegance and extra flavor.

Enjoy your Vanilla Panna Cotta Shake! It's a creamy, elegant treat that brings the delicate flavors of vanilla panna cotta into a refreshing and indulgent milkshake.

Pistachio Éclair Shake

Ingredients:

- 1 cup milk (dairy or non-dairy, such as almond or oat milk)
- 1/2 cup vanilla ice cream (or dairy-free vanilla ice cream)
- 1/2 cup Greek yogurt (plain or vanilla)
- 1/4 cup pistachio paste or pistachio cream (store-bought or homemade)
- 4-6 pistachio éclairs (store-bought or homemade, crumbled)
- 2 tablespoons caramel sauce (optional, for extra sweetness and flavor)
- 1/4 teaspoon vanilla extract
- Ice cubes (as needed)
- Optional: Whipped cream, chopped pistachios, and a drizzle of caramel sauce for garnish

Instructions:

1. **Prepare Pistachios:**
   - If using pistachio paste, ensure it's smooth and well-stirred. If using whole pistachios, you can blend them into a paste or cream in advance.
2. **Prepare Éclairs:**
   - If using store-bought or homemade pistachio éclairs, crumble them into small pieces.
3. **Blend Ingredients:**
   - In a blender, combine the milk, vanilla ice cream, Greek yogurt, pistachio paste, crumbled éclairs, caramel sauce (if using), and vanilla extract.
4. **Add Ice:**
   - Add a handful of ice cubes for a thicker, colder shake.
5. **Blend:**
   - Blend on high until smooth and creamy. If the shake is too thick, add more milk to reach your desired consistency.
6. **Taste and Adjust:**
   - Taste the shake and adjust sweetness or flavor if needed by adding more caramel sauce or pistachio paste.
7. **Serve:**
   - Pour the shake into a glass. Optionally, top with whipped cream, a sprinkle of chopped pistachios, and a drizzle of caramel sauce for a decorative and indulgent touch.

Enjoy your Pistachio Éclair Shake! It's a creamy and luxurious treat that brings the rich, nutty flavor of pistachios and the delightful taste of éclairs into a refreshing milkshake.

Crêpe Suzette Shake

Ingredients:

- 1 cup milk (dairy or non-dairy, such as almond or oat milk)
- 1/2 cup vanilla ice cream (or dairy-free vanilla ice cream)
- 1/2 cup Greek yogurt (plain or vanilla)
- 1/4 cup orange juice (freshly squeezed if possible)
- 2 tablespoons orange liqueur or orange extract (optional, for a more authentic flavor)
- 1 tablespoon sugar or honey (adjust to taste)
- 1/4 teaspoon vanilla extract
- 1 tablespoon melted butter (cooled)
- Ice cubes (as needed)
- Optional: Whipped cream, orange zest, and a drizzle of orange syrup for garnish

Instructions:

1. **Prepare Ingredients:**
   - If using orange liqueur, ensure it's suitable for your preference. If not using alcohol, orange extract can be used for flavor. Melt the butter and let it cool before using.
2. **Blend Ingredients:**
   - In a blender, combine the milk, vanilla ice cream, Greek yogurt, orange juice, orange liqueur (if using), sugar or honey, vanilla extract, and melted butter.
3. **Add Ice:**
   - Add a handful of ice cubes for a thicker, colder shake.
4. **Blend:**
   - Blend on high until smooth and creamy. If the shake is too thick, add more milk to reach your desired consistency.
5. **Taste and Adjust:**
   - Taste the shake and adjust sweetness or orange flavor if needed by adding more sugar or orange juice.
6. **Serve:**
   - Pour the shake into a glass. Optionally, top with whipped cream, a sprinkle of orange zest, and a drizzle of orange syrup for a decorative and indulgent touch.

Enjoy your Crêpe Suzette Shake! It's a creamy, citrusy treat that captures the classic flavors of Crêpe Suzette in a refreshing and indulgent milkshake.

French Toast Shake

Ingredients:

- 1 cup milk (dairy or non-dairy, such as almond or oat milk)
- 1/2 cup vanilla ice cream (or dairy-free vanilla ice cream)
- 1/2 cup Greek yogurt (plain or vanilla)
- 1-2 slices of French toast (freshly made or toasted; can be plain or slightly cinnamon-flavored)
- 1 tablespoon maple syrup
- 1/2 teaspoon ground cinnamon
- 1/4 teaspoon vanilla extract
- Ice cubes (as needed)
- Optional: Whipped cream, a sprinkle of cinnamon, and a drizzle of maple syrup for garnish

Instructions:

1. **Prepare French Toast:**
   - If using fresh French toast, allow it to cool slightly. You can toast it to make it a bit drier and easier to blend.
2. **Blend Ingredients:**
   - In a blender, combine the milk, vanilla ice cream, Greek yogurt, French toast slices, maple syrup, ground cinnamon, and vanilla extract.
3. **Add Ice:**
   - Add a handful of ice cubes for a thicker, colder shake.
4. **Blend:**
   - Blend on high until smooth and creamy. If the shake is too thick, add more milk to reach your desired consistency.
5. **Taste and Adjust:**
   - Taste the shake and adjust sweetness or cinnamon flavor if needed by adding more maple syrup or cinnamon.
6. **Serve:**
   - Pour the shake into a glass. Optionally, top with whipped cream, a sprinkle of cinnamon, and a drizzle of maple syrup for an extra indulgent touch.

Enjoy your French Toast Shake! It's a creamy, comforting treat that brings the flavors of French toast into a refreshing and indulgent milkshake.

Mango Madeleine Shake

Ingredients:

- 1 cup mango chunks (fresh or frozen)
- 1 cup vanilla ice cream
- 1/2 cup milk (you can adjust for desired thickness)
- 2-3 Madeleines (store-bought or homemade)
- 1 tablespoon honey or sugar (optional, depending on the sweetness of the mango)
- Ice cubes (optional, for extra thickness)

Instructions:

1. **Prepare the Ingredients:** If using fresh mango, peel and chop it into chunks. If using frozen mango, you can skip the ice cubes.
2. **Blend:** In a blender, combine the mango chunks, vanilla ice cream, milk, and honey or sugar (if using). Blend until smooth.
3. **Add Madeleines:** Break the Madeleines into pieces and add them to the blender. Blend again until the Madeleines are incorporated but still slightly chunky for texture.
4. **Adjust Consistency:** If the shake is too thick, add a little more milk and blend again. If it's too thin, add a few ice cubes and blend.
5. **Serve:** Pour the shake into glasses and enjoy immediately.

Feel free to get creative with the toppings—whipped cream, a sprinkle of cinnamon, or even a few extra crumbled Madeleines on top would be delightful!

Chocolat Praliné Shake

Ingredients:

- **1 cup chocolate ice cream** (or frozen yogurt for a lighter version)
- **1/2 cup milk** (dairy or non-dairy, adjust for desired thickness)
- **2 tablespoons praline paste** (you can find this at specialty stores or online; if not available, you can use praline syrup or make your own by blending toasted nuts with a bit of sugar)
- **1 tablespoon cocoa powder** (optional, for extra chocolatey flavor)
- **Whipped cream** (for topping)
- **Crushed praline nuts** or **chocolate shavings** (for garnish)

Instructions:

1. **Blend the Ingredients:**
    - In a blender, combine the chocolate ice cream, milk, and praline paste.
    - If you're using cocoa powder, add it to the blender for a richer chocolate flavor.
    - Blend until smooth and creamy. Adjust the consistency by adding more milk if it's too thick or a few ice cubes if you want it thicker.
2. **Serve:**
    - Pour the shake into glasses.
3. **Garnish:**
    - Top with a generous dollop of whipped cream.
    - Sprinkle with crushed praline nuts or chocolate shavings for a touch of elegance and extra flavor.

This shake combines the rich taste of chocolate with the nutty, caramelized flavor of praline, making it a truly indulgent treat. Enjoy!

Raspberry Sorbet Shake

Ingredients:

- **1 cup raspberry sorbet** (store-bought or homemade)
- **1/2 cup vanilla yogurt** (for creaminess; use dairy or non-dairy yogurt as preferred)
- **1/2 cup milk** (dairy or non-dairy; adjust for thickness)
- **1 tablespoon honey** or maple syrup (optional, for extra sweetness if needed)
- **Fresh raspberries** (for garnish)
- **Mint leaves** (optional, for garnish)

Instructions:

1. **Blend the Shake:**
   - In a blender, combine the raspberry sorbet, vanilla yogurt, and milk.
   - Blend until smooth. If the shake is too thick, add a little more milk and blend again. If it's too thin, add a few ice cubes or a bit more sorbet.
2. **Adjust Sweetness:**
   - Taste the shake. If you prefer it sweeter, add honey or maple syrup and blend briefly to mix.
3. **Serve:**
   - Pour the shake into glasses.
4. **Garnish:**
   - Garnish with fresh raspberries and a mint leaf if desired. You can also add a few extra spoonfuls of sorbet on top for extra texture and visual appeal.

This shake combines the tangy sweetness of raspberry sorbet with the creaminess of yogurt, creating a refreshing and delicious drink. Enjoy!

Peach Clafoutis Shake

Ingredients:

- **1 cup fresh or frozen peaches** (peeled, pitted, and chopped; if using frozen, let them thaw slightly)
- **1/2 cup vanilla ice cream** (or frozen yogurt for a lighter option)
- **1/2 cup milk** (dairy or non-dairy, adjust for desired thickness)
- **1/4 cup Greek yogurt** (for extra creaminess and a hint of tang)
- **1 tablespoon honey** or maple syrup (optional, for added sweetness)
- **1/4 teaspoon ground cinnamon** (optional, for a hint of spice)
- **1/4 teaspoon vanilla extract** (optional, for extra flavor)
- **1 tablespoon all-purpose flour** (to mimic the batter texture of clafoutis; optional but recommended for authenticity)
- **Crumbled Madeleines** or a sprinkle of powdered sugar (for garnish, optional)

Instructions:

1. **Prepare the Peaches:**
   - If using fresh peaches, peel, pit, and chop them. If using frozen peaches, let them thaw slightly for easier blending.
2. **Blend the Shake:**
   - In a blender, combine the peaches, vanilla ice cream, milk, Greek yogurt, and honey.
   - Add the ground cinnamon, vanilla extract, and all-purpose flour if using.
   - Blend until smooth and creamy. The flour helps add a slight texture reminiscent of clafoutis.
3. **Adjust Consistency:**
   - Check the consistency of the shake. If it's too thick, add a bit more milk and blend again. If it's too thin, add a few ice cubes or more ice cream.
4. **Serve:**
   - Pour the shake into glasses.
5. **Garnish:**
   - Optionally, top with crumbled Madeleines or a light dusting of powdered sugar for an elegant touch.

This shake brings the fruity sweetness of peaches and the comforting flavors of clafoutis into a creamy, drinkable form. Enjoy your unique and delicious Peach Clafoutis Shake!

Almond Croissant Shake

Ingredients:

- **1 almond croissant** (store-bought or homemade)
- **1 cup vanilla ice cream** (or almond-flavored ice cream if you prefer a stronger almond taste)
- **1/2 cup milk** (dairy or non-dairy, adjust for thickness)
- **1/4 cup Greek yogurt** (for extra creaminess)
- **1 tablespoon almond butter** (for added almond flavor; optional)
- **1 tablespoon honey** or maple syrup (optional, for extra sweetness)
- **Crushed almonds** or **toasted almond slices** (for garnish)
- **Whipped cream** (optional, for topping)

Instructions:

1. **Prepare the Croissant:**
   - Tear the almond croissant into chunks. If you want to enhance the flavor, you can lightly toast the pieces before adding them to the blender.
2. **Blend the Shake:**
   - In a blender, combine the croissant chunks, vanilla ice cream, milk, Greek yogurt, and almond butter (if using).
   - Blend until smooth and creamy. If the shake is too thick, add a little more milk. If it's too thin, add more ice cream or a few ice cubes.
3. **Adjust Sweetness:**
   - Taste the shake and add honey or maple syrup if you prefer it sweeter. Blend again briefly to mix.
4. **Serve:**
   - Pour the shake into glasses.
5. **Garnish:**
   - Top with whipped cream, if desired.
   - Sprinkle with crushed almonds or toasted almond slices for added texture and flavor.

This shake offers the rich, nutty flavors of an almond croissant in a creamy, drinkable form. It's a deliciously indulgent treat that's sure to satisfy. Enjoy!

Lemon Meringue Shake

Ingredients:

- **1 cup vanilla ice cream** (or lemon sorbet for a lighter, tangier option)
- **1/2 cup milk** (dairy or non-dairy, adjust for desired thickness)
- **1/4 cup lemon curd** (store-bought or homemade for intense lemon flavor)
- **1 tablespoon lemon juice** (for extra tanginess)
- **1/2 teaspoon vanilla extract** (optional, for added depth of flavor)
- **Whipped cream** (for topping)
- **Crushed meringue cookies** or **lemon zest** (for garnish)

Instructions:

1. **Blend the Shake:**
    - In a blender, combine the vanilla ice cream, milk, lemon curd, and lemon juice.
    - Add the vanilla extract if using.
    - Blend until smooth and creamy. If the shake is too thick, add a little more milk. If it's too thin, add more ice cream.
2. **Serve:**
    - Pour the shake into glasses.
3. **Garnish:**
    - Top with a generous dollop of whipped cream.
    - Sprinkle crushed meringue cookies or lemon zest on top for added texture and flavor.

This shake captures the essence of lemon meringue pie in a creamy, drinkable form. It's a perfect balance of tart lemon and sweet, creamy meringue flavors. Enjoy!

Brioche and Jam Shake

Ingredients:

- **1 cup brioche bread** (cut into chunks; lightly toasted for extra flavor if desired)
- **1 cup vanilla ice cream** (or use a flavor like caramel for added richness)
- **1/2 cup milk** (dairy or non-dairy, adjust for thickness)
- **1/4 cup fruit jam** (such as raspberry, strawberry, or apricot; choose your favorite)
- **1/4 cup Greek yogurt** (for extra creaminess)
- **1 tablespoon honey** or maple syrup (optional, for added sweetness)
- **Whipped cream** (for topping)
- **Additional jam** (for drizzle or swirl, optional)
- **Crushed brioche or toast crumbs** (for garnish, optional)

Instructions:

1. **Prepare the Brioche:**
    - Cut the brioche into chunks. If you like, lightly toast them for a bit of extra flavor and texture.
2. **Blend the Shake:**
    - In a blender, combine the brioche chunks, vanilla ice cream, milk, fruit jam, and Greek yogurt.
    - Blend until smooth and creamy. If the shake is too thick, add more milk. If it's too thin, add more ice cream or a few ice cubes.
3. **Adjust Sweetness:**
    - Taste the shake. If you'd like it sweeter, add honey or maple syrup and blend briefly.
4. **Serve:**
    - Pour the shake into glasses.
5. **Garnish:**
    - Top with whipped cream.
    - Optionally, drizzle with additional jam or swirl it into the whipped cream.
    - Sprinkle with crushed brioche or toast crumbs for added texture and visual appeal.

This shake offers a delicious blend of buttery brioche and sweet jam, creating a dessert that's both comforting and indulgent. Enjoy!

Profiterole Shake

Ingredients:

- **1 cup vanilla ice cream** (or use a flavor like chocolate for extra richness)
- **1/2 cup milk** (dairy or non-dairy, adjust for thickness)
- **1/4 cup cream puffs** (store-bought or homemade; for authenticity, use plain or lightly sweetened cream puffs)
- **2 tablespoons chocolate sauce** (store-bought or homemade)
- **1/4 cup whipped cream** (optional, for a richer texture)
- **1 tablespoon powdered sugar** (optional, for added sweetness)
- **Crushed nuts** (like almonds or hazelnuts, optional, for garnish)
- **Extra chocolate sauce** (for drizzling on top)

Instructions:

1. **Prepare the Cream Puffs:**
    - If using store-bought cream puffs, you can lightly toast them for added texture if desired.
2. **Blend the Shake:**
    - In a blender, combine the vanilla ice cream, milk, and cream puffs.
    - Blend until smooth and creamy. If the shake is too thick, add more milk. If it's too thin, add more ice cream or a few ice cubes.
3. **Add Chocolate Sauce:**
    - Add 2 tablespoons of chocolate sauce to the blender and blend briefly to mix in the chocolate flavor. If you prefer, you can swirl the chocolate sauce into the shake instead of blending it.
4. **Serve:**
    - Pour the shake into glasses.
5. **Garnish:**
    - Top with a dollop of whipped cream if using.
    - Drizzle extra chocolate sauce over the whipped cream.
    - Sprinkle with crushed nuts for added texture and flavor.

This shake combines the creamy, pastry-like elements of profiteroles with rich chocolate, making it a decadent and delightful treat. Enjoy your Profiterole Shake!

Nutella Crêpe Shake

Ingredients:

- **1 cup vanilla ice cream** (or chocolate ice cream for a richer flavor)
- **1/2 cup milk** (dairy or non-dairy, adjust for thickness)
- **2 tablespoons Nutella** (or more if you like it extra chocolaty)
- **1 crêpe** (store-bought or homemade, cut into pieces; you can use a plain crêpe or one with a bit of sugar)
- **1/4 cup Greek yogurt** (for extra creaminess)
- **1 tablespoon honey** or maple syrup (optional, for added sweetness)
- **Whipped cream** (for topping)
- **Extra Nutella** (for drizzling)
- **Powdered sugar** (for garnish, optional)

Instructions:

1. **Prepare the Crêpe:**
   - If using homemade crêpes, make sure they are cooled and cut into small pieces. Store-bought crêpes work fine too.
2. **Blend the Shake:**
   - In a blender, combine the vanilla ice cream, milk, Nutella, crêpe pieces, and Greek yogurt.
   - Blend until smooth and creamy. If the shake is too thick, add more milk. If it's too thin, add more ice cream or a few ice cubes.
3. **Adjust Sweetness:**
   - Taste the shake and add honey or maple syrup if you prefer it sweeter. Blend again briefly to mix.
4. **Serve:**
   - Pour the shake into glasses.
5. **Garnish:**
   - Top with whipped cream.
   - Drizzle extra Nutella over the whipped cream.
   - Optionally, dust with powdered sugar for a touch of elegance.

This shake combines the creamy richness of Nutella with the buttery flavor of crêpes, creating a decadent and satisfying treat. Enjoy your Nutella Crêpe Shake!

Lavender Honey Shake

Ingredients:

- **1 cup vanilla ice cream** (or a mild-flavored ice cream like honey or lavender for added depth)
- **1/2 cup milk** (dairy or non-dairy, adjust for thickness)
- **1 tablespoon honey** (preferably a good-quality, floral honey)
- **1/2 teaspoon dried lavender buds** (culinary grade; or you can use lavender syrup for a stronger flavor)
- **1/4 teaspoon vanilla extract** (optional, for added depth)
- **Whipped cream** (for topping, optional)
- **Additional honey** (for drizzling)
- **Lavender buds** (for garnish, optional)

Instructions:

1. **Infuse the Lavender:**
    - If using dried lavender buds, gently heat the milk in a small saucepan over low heat. Add the lavender buds and let them steep for about 5 minutes. Strain out the lavender buds and let the milk cool to room temperature. If using lavender syrup, skip this step and add the syrup directly to the blender.
2. **Blend the Shake:**
    - In a blender, combine the cooled lavender-infused milk (or lavender syrup), vanilla ice cream, honey, and vanilla extract if using.
    - Blend until smooth and creamy. If the shake is too thick, add a bit more milk. If it's too thin, add a few ice cubes or more ice cream.
3. **Serve:**
    - Pour the shake into glasses.
4. **Garnish:**
    - Top with whipped cream if desired.
    - Drizzle additional honey over the whipped cream.
    - Sprinkle with a few lavender buds for a decorative touch.

This shake combines the floral aroma of lavender with the sweet richness of honey, creating a unique and comforting flavor profile. Enjoy your Lavender Honey Shake!

Cassis Shake

Ingredients:

- **1 cup vanilla ice cream** (or yogurt for a lighter option)
- **1/2 cup milk** (dairy or non-dairy, adjust for desired thickness)
- **1/4 cup blackcurrant syrup** or **blackcurrant puree** (available in specialty stores or online)
- **1 tablespoon honey** or maple syrup (optional, for added sweetness)
- **1/4 teaspoon lemon juice** (to balance the flavor, optional)
- **Whipped cream** (for topping, optional)
- **Fresh blackcurrants** or **blackcurrant compote** (for garnish, optional)

Instructions:

1. **Blend the Shake:**
    - In a blender, combine the vanilla ice cream, milk, blackcurrant syrup or puree, and honey (if using).
    - Blend until smooth and creamy. If the shake is too thick, add a bit more milk. If it's too thin, add more ice cream or a few ice cubes.
2. **Adjust Flavor:**
    - Taste the shake and adjust the sweetness with honey or maple syrup if needed. Add a splash of lemon juice if you want to enhance the tartness.
3. **Serve:**
    - Pour the shake into glasses.
4. **Garnish:**
    - Top with whipped cream if desired.
    - Garnish with fresh blackcurrants or a spoonful of blackcurrant compote for extra flavor and visual appeal.

This shake offers a rich, fruity flavor with a touch of sweetness and tanginess, perfect for a refreshing treat. Enjoy your Cassis Shake!

Apple Tartelette Shake

Ingredients:

- **1 cup vanilla ice cream** (or cinnamon ice cream for extra flavor)
- **1/2 cup milk** (dairy or non-dairy, adjust for desired thickness)
- **1/2 cup apple pie filling** or **apple compote** (store-bought or homemade; for a more authentic flavor, use apple pie filling with chunks of apple)
- **1/4 teaspoon ground cinnamon** (optional, for extra spice)
- **1/4 teaspoon vanilla extract** (optional, for added depth)
- **1 tablespoon caramel sauce** (optional, for added sweetness and richness)
- **Whipped cream** (for topping, optional)
- **Crumpled pie crust** or **toasted almond slices** (for garnish, optional)

Instructions:

1. **Blend the Shake:**
    - In a blender, combine the vanilla ice cream, milk, and apple pie filling or apple compote.
    - Add ground cinnamon and vanilla extract if using.
    - Blend until smooth and creamy. If the shake is too thick, add more milk. If it's too thin, add more ice cream or a few ice cubes.
2. **Adjust Flavor:**
    - Taste the shake and adjust the sweetness with caramel sauce if desired. Blend briefly to mix.
3. **Serve:**
    - Pour the shake into glasses.
4. **Garnish:**
    - Top with whipped cream if desired.
    - Sprinkle crumbled pie crust or toasted almond slices on top for added texture and flavor.

This shake offers the comforting flavors of an apple tartelette with the creamy indulgence of a milkshake. It's perfect for a special treat or a cozy dessert. Enjoy!

Café au Lait Crème Shake

Ingredients:

- **1 cup vanilla ice cream** (or coffee-flavored ice cream for a stronger coffee taste)
- **1/2 cup brewed coffee** (cooled; use strong coffee for a more intense flavor)
- **1/2 cup milk** (dairy or non-dairy; adjust for desired thickness)
- **1/4 cup whipped cream** (for added creaminess and texture)
- **1 tablespoon sugar** or **simple syrup** (optional, for added sweetness)
- **1/4 teaspoon vanilla extract** (optional, for extra depth)
- **Cinnamon** or **cocoa powder** (for garnish, optional)
- **Chocolate shavings** or **coffee beans** (for garnish, optional)

Instructions:

1. **Prepare the Coffee:**
    - Brew your coffee and let it cool to room temperature. For the best flavor, use a strong brew.
2. **Blend the Shake:**
    - In a blender, combine the vanilla ice cream, cooled coffee, milk, and whipped cream.
    - Add sugar or simple syrup if you prefer a sweeter shake, and vanilla extract if using.
    - Blend until smooth and creamy. If the shake is too thick, add a bit more milk. If it's too thin, add more ice cream or a few ice cubes.
3. **Serve:**
    - Pour the shake into glasses.
4. **Garnish:**
    - Top with a dollop of whipped cream.
    - Sprinkle with a dash of cinnamon or cocoa powder for extra flavor.
    - Optionally, garnish with chocolate shavings or coffee beans for a decorative touch.

This shake brings together the bold taste of coffee with the creamy sweetness of a milkshake, creating a delightful and refreshing treat. Enjoy your Café au Lait Crème Shake!

Gingerbread Macaron Shake

Ingredients:

- **1 cup vanilla ice cream** (or gingerbread-flavored ice cream if available)
- **1/2 cup milk** (dairy or non-dairy, adjust for thickness)
- **1/4 cup gingerbread syrup** or **gingerbread cookies** (crushed; for a more intense flavor, use gingerbread syrup or gingerbread cookie crumbs)
- **1/4 teaspoon ground ginger** (optional, for extra spice)
- **1/4 teaspoon ground cinnamon** (optional, for added warmth)
- **1/4 teaspoon vanilla extract** (optional, for depth of flavor)
- **Whipped cream** (for topping)
- **Crushed macarons** or **gingerbread cookie crumbs** (for garnish, optional)
- **Caramel sauce** or **chocolate sauce** (for drizzling, optional)

Instructions:

1. **Prepare the Ingredients:**
   - If using gingerbread cookies, crush them into small pieces or crumbs.
   - If using gingerbread syrup, measure it out.
2. **Blend the Shake:**
   - In a blender, combine the vanilla ice cream, milk, gingerbread syrup or crushed gingerbread cookies, and optional ground ginger, ground cinnamon, and vanilla extract.
   - Blend until smooth and creamy. If the shake is too thick, add a bit more milk. If it's too thin, add more ice cream or a few ice cubes.
3. **Serve:**
   - Pour the shake into glasses.
4. **Garnish:**
   - Top with a generous dollop of whipped cream.
   - Sprinkle with crushed macarons or gingerbread cookie crumbs.
   - Drizzle with caramel sauce or chocolate sauce for extra sweetness and visual appeal.

This shake blends the festive flavors of gingerbread with the elegant sweetness of macarons, creating a deliciously unique treat. Enjoy your Gingerbread Macaron Shake!

Chardonnay Peach Shake

Ingredients:

- **1 cup vanilla ice cream** (or peach ice cream for enhanced flavor)
- **1/2 cup milk** (dairy or non-dairy, adjust for thickness)
- **1/2 cup fresh or frozen peaches** (peeled and pitted; if using frozen, let them thaw slightly)
- **1/4 cup Chardonnay** (or other dry white wine; optional and for adults only)
- **1 tablespoon honey** or maple syrup (optional, for extra sweetness)
- **1/4 teaspoon vanilla extract** (optional, for added depth of flavor)
- **Whipped cream** (for topping, optional)
- **Peach slices** or **mint leaves** (for garnish, optional)

Instructions:

1. **Prepare the Peaches:**
   - If using fresh peaches, peel, pit, and chop them. If using frozen peaches, let them thaw slightly to make blending easier.
2. **Blend the Shake:**
   - In a blender, combine the vanilla ice cream, milk, peaches, and Chardonnay.
   - Add honey or maple syrup if you prefer a sweeter shake.
   - Blend until smooth and creamy. If the shake is too thick, add more milk. If it's too thin, add more ice cream or a few ice cubes.
3. **Adjust Flavor:**
   - Taste the shake and adjust the sweetness or add more Chardonnay if desired. Blend again briefly to mix.
4. **Serve:**
   - Pour the shake into glasses.
5. **Garnish:**
   - Top with whipped cream if desired.
   - Garnish with peach slices or a sprig of mint for a fresh and attractive finish.

This shake combines the sweet and juicy flavor of peaches with the subtle notes of Chardonnay, making for a refreshing and elegant treat. Enjoy your Chardonnay Peach Shake!

Vanilla Bean Crêpe Shake

Ingredients:

- **1 cup vanilla bean ice cream** (or plain vanilla ice cream if vanilla bean isn't available)
- **1/2 cup milk** (dairy or non-dairy, adjust for thickness)
- **1 crêpe** (store-bought or homemade; plain or lightly sweetened; cut into pieces)
- **1/4 cup vanilla yogurt** (for added creaminess)
- **1 tablespoon honey** or maple syrup (optional, for added sweetness)
- **1/4 teaspoon vanilla extract** (optional, for extra vanilla flavor)
- **Whipped cream** (for topping, optional)
- **Powdered sugar** (for garnish, optional)
- **Additional crêpe pieces** or **vanilla bean paste** (for garnish, optional)

Instructions:

1. **Prepare the Crêpe:**
   - If using homemade crêpes, ensure they are cooled and cut into small pieces. Store-bought crêpes work well too.
2. **Blend the Shake:**
   - In a blender, combine the vanilla bean ice cream, milk, crêpe pieces, and vanilla yogurt.
   - Add honey or maple syrup if you prefer a sweeter shake, and vanilla extract if using.
   - Blend until smooth and creamy. If the shake is too thick, add a bit more milk. If it's too thin, add more ice cream or a few ice cubes.
3. **Serve:**
   - Pour the shake into glasses.
4. **Garnish:**
   - Top with whipped cream if desired.
   - Sprinkle with powdered sugar for a touch of elegance.
   - Garnish with additional crêpe pieces or a swirl of vanilla bean paste for extra flavor and visual appeal.

This shake combines the creamy sweetness of vanilla bean with the buttery flavor of crêpes, creating a decadent and satisfying treat. Enjoy your Vanilla Bean Crêpe Shake!

Berry Compote Shake

Ingredients:

For the Berry Compote:

- **1 cup mixed berries** (fresh or frozen; such as strawberries, blueberries, raspberries, and blackberries)
- **2 tablespoons sugar** (or to taste)
- **1 tablespoon lemon juice** (for a hint of brightness)
- **1 teaspoon vanilla extract** (optional)

For the Shake:

- **1 cup vanilla ice cream** (or berry-flavored ice cream for a more intense berry flavor)
- **1/2 cup milk** (dairy or non-dairy, adjust for thickness)
- **1/4 cup berry compote** (cooled; adjust amount for desired berry flavor)
- **Whipped cream** (for topping, optional)
- **Additional berries** or **compote** (for garnish, optional)
- **Mint leaves** (for garnish, optional)

Instructions:

1. **Prepare the Berry Compote:**
    - In a saucepan over medium heat, combine the mixed berries, sugar, and lemon juice.
    - Cook, stirring occasionally, until the berries break down and the mixture thickens slightly (about 10-15 minutes). If using fresh berries, you may need to cook longer to achieve the desired consistency.
    - Remove from heat and stir in vanilla extract if using. Let the compote cool to room temperature. You can store it in the refrigerator if making ahead.
2. **Blend the Shake:**
    - In a blender, combine the vanilla ice cream, milk, and 1/4 cup of the cooled berry compote.
    - Blend until smooth and creamy. If the shake is too thick, add more milk. If it's too thin, add more ice cream or a few ice cubes.
3. **Serve:**
    - Pour the shake into glasses.
4. **Garnish:**
    - Top with whipped cream if desired.
    - Drizzle additional berry compote over the whipped cream.
    - Garnish with fresh berries or a sprig of mint for a fresh touch.

This shake combines the creamy richness of vanilla ice cream with the sweet-tart flavors of berry compote, creating a refreshing and delicious treat. Enjoy your Berry Compote Shake!

Chocolate Hazelnut Croissant Shake

Ingredients:

- **1 chocolate croissant** (or a plain croissant with chocolate spread, cut into chunks; lightly toasted for extra flavor if desired)
- **1 cup vanilla ice cream** (or chocolate ice cream for extra richness)
- **1/2 cup milk** (dairy or non-dairy, adjust for thickness)
- **2 tablespoons chocolate hazelnut spread** (such as Nutella)
- **1/4 cup Greek yogurt** (for added creaminess)
- **1 tablespoon honey** or maple syrup (optional, for added sweetness)
- **Whipped cream** (for topping, optional)
- **Chocolate shavings** or **crushed hazelnuts** (for garnish, optional)
- **Extra chocolate hazelnut spread** (for drizzling, optional)

Instructions:

1. **Prepare the Croissant:**
   - Cut the chocolate croissant into chunks. If you like, you can lightly toast the chunks to add extra flavor and texture.
2. **Blend the Shake:**
   - In a blender, combine the croissant chunks, vanilla ice cream, milk, chocolate hazelnut spread, and Greek yogurt.
   - Blend until smooth and creamy. If the shake is too thick, add a bit more milk. If it's too thin, add more ice cream or a few ice cubes.
3. **Adjust Sweetness:**
   - Taste the shake and add honey or maple syrup if you prefer it sweeter. Blend briefly to mix.
4. **Serve:**
   - Pour the shake into glasses.
5. **Garnish:**
   - Top with whipped cream if desired.
   - Drizzle extra chocolate hazelnut spread over the whipped cream.
   - Sprinkle with chocolate shavings or crushed hazelnuts for added texture and visual appeal.

This shake combines the rich, nutty flavors of hazelnuts and chocolate with the buttery goodness of a croissant, creating a luxurious and satisfying treat. Enjoy your Chocolate Hazelnut Croissant Shake!

Lemon Basil Shake

Ingredients:

- **1 cup vanilla ice cream** (or lemon sorbet for a lighter, tangy option)
- **1/2 cup milk** (dairy or non-dairy, adjust for thickness)
- **1/4 cup fresh lemon juice** (about 1 lemon)
- **1 tablespoon lemon zest** (for extra lemon flavor)
- **1/4 cup fresh basil leaves** (tightly packed)
- **1 tablespoon honey** or maple syrup (optional, for added sweetness)
- **Whipped cream** (for topping, optional)
- **Additional lemon zest** or **fresh basil leaves** (for garnish, optional)

Instructions:

1. **Prepare the Basil:**
    - Lightly bruise the basil leaves by gently crushing them with the back of a spoon or a muddler. This helps to release their flavor.
2. **Blend the Shake:**
    - In a blender, combine the vanilla ice cream, milk, fresh lemon juice, lemon zest, and basil leaves.
    - Add honey or maple syrup if you prefer a sweeter shake.
    - Blend until smooth and creamy. If the shake is too thick, add a bit more milk. If it's too thin, add more ice cream or a few ice cubes.
3. **Serve:**
    - Pour the shake into glasses.
4. **Garnish:**
    - Top with whipped cream if desired.
    - Garnish with additional lemon zest or a sprig of fresh basil for a refreshing and decorative touch.

This shake combines the tangy brightness of lemon with the aromatic freshness of basil, creating a unique and invigorating flavor experience. Enjoy your Lemon Basil Shake!

Raspberry Ganache Shake

Ingredients:

For the Ganache:

- **1/2 cup heavy cream**
- **1/2 cup semisweet or bittersweet chocolate chips** (or finely chopped chocolate)
- **1 tablespoon raspberry liqueur** (optional, for enhanced raspberry flavor; can substitute with 1 tablespoon of raspberry syrup)

For the Shake:

- **1 cup vanilla ice cream** (or chocolate ice cream for extra richness)
- **1/2 cup milk** (dairy or non-dairy, adjust for thickness)
- **1/2 cup fresh or frozen raspberries** (thawed if frozen)
- **1/4 cup raspberry syrup** (optional, for extra raspberry flavor)
- **Whipped cream** (for topping, optional)
- **Additional ganache** (for drizzling, optional)
- **Fresh raspberries** or **chocolate shavings** (for garnish, optional)

Instructions:

1. **Make the Ganache:**
    - Heat the heavy cream in a small saucepan over medium heat until it starts to simmer.
    - Remove from heat and add the chocolate chips. Stir until the chocolate is completely melted and smooth.
    - If using, stir in the raspberry liqueur or raspberry syrup. Let the ganache cool to room temperature.
2. **Blend the Shake:**
    - In a blender, combine the vanilla ice cream, milk, fresh or frozen raspberries, and raspberry syrup (if using).
    - Add 1/4 cup of the cooled ganache to the blender.
    - Blend until smooth and creamy. If the shake is too thick, add more milk. If it's too thin, add more ice cream or a few ice cubes.
3. **Serve:**
    - Pour the shake into glasses.
4. **Garnish:**
    - Top with whipped cream if desired.
    - Drizzle additional ganache over the whipped cream.
    - Garnish with fresh raspberries or chocolate shavings for added texture and a touch of elegance.

This shake combines the rich, smooth flavor of chocolate ganache with the tart and refreshing taste of raspberries, creating a dessert that's both indulgent and satisfying. Enjoy your Raspberry Ganache Shake!

Honey Almond Shake

Ingredients:

- **1 cup vanilla ice cream** (or almond-flavored ice cream for a more intense almond flavor)
- **1/2 cup milk** (dairy or non-dairy, adjust for thickness)
- **2 tablespoons almond butter** (or almond paste for a more intense almond flavor)
- **1-2 tablespoons honey** (to taste)
- **1/4 teaspoon almond extract** (optional, for extra almond flavor)
- **Whipped cream** (for topping, optional)
- **Chopped almonds** or **toasted almond slices** (for garnish, optional)
- **Additional honey** (for drizzling, optional)

Instructions:

1. **Blend the Shake:**
   - In a blender, combine the vanilla ice cream, milk, almond butter, and honey.
   - Add almond extract if using.
   - Blend until smooth and creamy. If the shake is too thick, add more milk. If it's too thin, add more ice cream or a few ice cubes.
2. **Adjust Sweetness:**
   - Taste the shake and adjust the sweetness by adding more honey if needed. Blend again briefly to mix.
3. **Serve:**
   - Pour the shake into glasses.
4. **Garnish:**
   - Top with whipped cream if desired.
   - Drizzle with additional honey.
   - Sprinkle with chopped almonds or toasted almond slices for added texture and visual appeal.

This shake brings together the smooth, nutty flavor of almonds with the sweet, golden notes of honey, creating a creamy and satisfying treat. Enjoy your Honey Almond Shake!

Pear Clafoutis Shake

Ingredients:

- 2 ripe pears, peeled, cored, and chopped
- 1/2 cup Greek yogurt (plain or vanilla)
- 1/2 cup milk (or a dairy-free alternative like almond or oat milk)
- 1/4 cup flour (all-purpose or a gluten-free alternative)
- 2 tablespoons honey or maple syrup (adjust to taste)
- 1/2 teaspoon vanilla extract
- 1/4 teaspoon ground cinnamon
- 1/4 teaspoon ground nutmeg
- A pinch of salt
- 1/2 cup ice (optional, for a colder, thicker shake)
- A handful of granola or crushed nuts (optional, for garnish)

Instructions:

1. **Prepare the Pears:**
   - Chop the pears into small pieces. You can either use them raw for a fresh flavor or cook them lightly in a pan with a bit of cinnamon and honey to enhance their sweetness and flavor. Let them cool if you cook them.
2. **Blend Ingredients:**
   - In a blender, combine the chopped pears, Greek yogurt, milk, flour, honey (or maple syrup), vanilla extract, cinnamon, nutmeg, and a pinch of salt.
   - Blend until smooth. If you prefer a thicker consistency, add ice and blend again.
3. **Taste and Adjust:**
   - Taste the shake and adjust the sweetness or spice levels as desired. If it's too thick, you can add a bit more milk to reach your preferred consistency.
4. **Serve:**
   - Pour the shake into glasses. If desired, top with granola or crushed nuts for added texture and a touch of crunch.
5. **Garnish (Optional):**
   - You can also sprinkle a bit more cinnamon or a drizzle of honey on top for extra flavor.

Enjoy your Pear Clafoutis Shake! It's a creative way to enjoy the flavors of clafoutis in a refreshing drink.

Orange Blossom Shake

Ingredients:

- 1 large orange, peeled and segmented (or 1 cup orange juice)
- 1/2 cup Greek yogurt (plain or vanilla)
- 1/2 cup milk (or a dairy-free alternative like almond or oat milk)
- 2 tablespoons honey or agave syrup (adjust to taste)
- 1/2 teaspoon orange blossom water
- 1/4 teaspoon vanilla extract
- 1/4 teaspoon ground cinnamon (optional, for a hint of warmth)
- 1/2 cup ice (optional, for a colder, thicker shake)
- Orange zest or a few slices of orange (for garnish)

Instructions:

1. **Prepare the Orange:**
   - If using fresh orange segments, peel and segment the orange, removing any seeds. If using orange juice, you can skip this step.
2. **Blend Ingredients:**
   - In a blender, combine the orange segments (or orange juice), Greek yogurt, milk, honey (or agave syrup), orange blossom water, vanilla extract, and ground cinnamon if using.
   - Blend until smooth. If you like a thicker shake, add ice and blend again.
3. **Taste and Adjust:**
   - Taste the shake and adjust the sweetness or orange blossom water if needed. Be cautious with the orange blossom water, as a little goes a long way.
4. **Serve:**
   - Pour the shake into glasses. Garnish with a bit of orange zest or a slice of orange for a touch of elegance.
5. **Enjoy:**
   - Serve immediately and enjoy the refreshing, floral flavors!

This Orange Blossom Shake is perfect for a sunny day or as a special treat. The orange blossom water adds a lovely, aromatic twist that sets it apart from more traditional shakes.

Banana Chocolate Croissant Shake

Ingredients:

- 1 ripe banana, peeled and sliced
- 1 cup milk (or a dairy-free alternative like almond or oat milk)
- 1/2 cup Greek yogurt (plain or vanilla)
- 1/4 cup chocolate syrup or melted dark chocolate
- 1/2 cup of croissant, torn into small pieces (preferably chocolate croissant, but a regular one will work too)
- 1-2 tablespoons honey or maple syrup (optional, adjust to taste)
- 1/2 teaspoon vanilla extract
- A pinch of salt
- 1/2 cup ice (optional, for a colder, thicker shake)
- Whipped cream and chocolate shavings (optional, for garnish)

Instructions:

1. **Prepare the Croissant:**
    - Tear the croissant into small pieces. If it's a plain croissant and you want a richer chocolate flavor, you can mix in a tablespoon of cocoa powder or a bit of chocolate syrup.
2. **Blend Ingredients:**
    - In a blender, combine the banana, milk, Greek yogurt, chocolate syrup (or melted chocolate), croissant pieces, honey (or maple syrup), vanilla extract, and a pinch of salt.
    - Blend until smooth. If you prefer a thicker shake, add ice and blend again.
3. **Taste and Adjust:**
    - Taste the shake and adjust the sweetness or chocolate level as needed. You can add more honey or syrup if you like it sweeter or more chocolate syrup for a richer flavor.
4. **Serve:**
    - Pour the shake into glasses. If desired, top with whipped cream and a sprinkle of chocolate shavings for an extra touch of indulgence.
5. **Enjoy:**
    - Serve immediately and savor the rich, chocolatey, and banana-filled goodness!

This shake brings together the best of a classic croissant with the creamy textures of a banana and chocolate treat. It's perfect for a special breakfast or a decadent dessert!

Crème Fraîche Shake

Ingredients:

- 1/2 cup crème fraîche
- 1/2 cup Greek yogurt (plain or vanilla)
- 1/2 cup milk (or a dairy-free alternative like almond or oat milk)
- 2 tablespoons honey or maple syrup (adjust to taste)
- 1/2 teaspoon vanilla extract
- 1/2 cup fruit of choice (e.g., berries, peaches, mango, or banana)
- A pinch of salt
- 1/2 cup ice (optional, for a colder, thicker shake)
- Fresh fruit or a mint sprig for garnish (optional)

Instructions:

1. **Prepare the Fruit:**
   - If using fresh fruit, wash and chop it into smaller pieces. If using frozen fruit, you can add it directly to the blender.
2. **Blend Ingredients:**
   - In a blender, combine the crème fraîche, Greek yogurt, milk, honey (or maple syrup), vanilla extract, fruit, and a pinch of salt.
   - Blend until smooth. If you prefer a thicker shake, add ice and blend again.
3. **Taste and Adjust:**
   - Taste the shake and adjust the sweetness or fruit quantity as needed. If it's too thick, you can add a bit more milk to reach your desired consistency.
4. **Serve:**
   - Pour the shake into glasses. Garnish with fresh fruit or a mint sprig if desired.
5. **Enjoy:**
   - Serve immediately and enjoy the creamy, tangy, and fruity flavors!

This Crème Fraîche Shake is versatile and can be adapted to include your favorite fruits or flavorings. The crème fraîche adds a luxurious, tangy creaminess that makes it stand out from a standard milkshake.

Strawberry Mille-Feuille Shake

Ingredients:

- 1 cup fresh or frozen strawberries (hulled)
- 1/2 cup crème fraîche (or Greek yogurt for a lighter option)
- 1/2 cup milk (or a dairy-free alternative like almond or oat milk)
- 1/4 cup puff pastry pieces (store-bought or homemade, broken into small pieces)
- 2 tablespoons honey or maple syrup (adjust to taste)
- 1/2 teaspoon vanilla extract
- 1/4 teaspoon ground cinnamon (optional, for a hint of warmth)
- A pinch of salt
- 1/2 cup ice (optional, for a colder, thicker shake)
- Whipped cream and additional puff pastry pieces for garnish (optional)

Instructions:

1. **Prepare the Strawberries:**
   - If using fresh strawberries, wash and hull them. If using frozen strawberries, you can add them directly to the blender.
2. **Blend Ingredients:**
   - In a blender, combine the strawberries, crème fraîche (or Greek yogurt), milk, puff pastry pieces, honey (or maple syrup), vanilla extract, ground cinnamon (if using), and a pinch of salt.
   - Blend until smooth. If you prefer a thicker consistency, add ice and blend again.
3. **Taste and Adjust:**
   - Taste the shake and adjust the sweetness or flavor as needed. You can add more honey or syrup if you like it sweeter.
4. **Serve:**
   - Pour the shake into glasses. For an extra touch, top with whipped cream and sprinkle additional puff pastry pieces on top for a bit of crunch.
5. **Enjoy:**
   - Serve immediately and enjoy the rich, creamy, and fruity flavors of this decadent shake!

This Strawberry Mille-Feuille Shake brings together the fresh, sweet flavor of strawberries with the crispy, buttery notes of puff pastry, creating a delightful twist on a traditional shake.

Bordeaux Wine Shake

Ingredients:

- 1/2 cup Bordeaux wine (or a similar red wine, preferably with fruity or earthy notes)
- 1 cup vanilla ice cream (or a dairy-free alternative)
- 1/2 cup milk (or a dairy-free alternative like almond or oat milk)
- 1/4 cup Greek yogurt (plain or vanilla, for extra creaminess)
- 1 tablespoon honey or maple syrup (adjust to taste)
- 1/2 teaspoon vanilla extract
- A pinch of salt
- 1/2 cup ice (optional, for a colder, thicker shake)
- Cocoa powder or shaved chocolate for garnish (optional)

Instructions:

1. **Prepare the Ingredients:**
   - Make sure the Bordeaux wine is chilled for the best flavor and texture in your shake.
2. **Blend Ingredients:**
   - In a blender, combine the Bordeaux wine, vanilla ice cream, milk, Greek yogurt, honey (or maple syrup), vanilla extract, and a pinch of salt.
   - Blend until smooth. If you like a thicker shake, add ice and blend again.
3. **Taste and Adjust:**
   - Taste the shake and adjust the sweetness or wine level as needed. You can add a bit more honey or syrup if you prefer a sweeter shake.
4. **Serve:**
   - Pour the shake into glasses. For a touch of elegance, sprinkle with cocoa powder or shaved chocolate on top.
5. **Enjoy:**
   - Serve immediately and savor the sophisticated blend of flavors!

Note: Since this shake contains alcohol, it's best enjoyed by adults. The Bordeaux wine adds a depth of flavor and richness that pairs beautifully with the creaminess of the ice cream and yogurt.

Creme Caramel Shake

Ingredients:

- 1/2 cup crème caramel or caramel flan (store-bought or homemade, chilled)
- 1 cup vanilla ice cream (or a dairy-free alternative)
- 1/2 cup milk (or a dairy-free alternative like almond or oat milk)
- 2 tablespoons caramel sauce (plus extra for drizzling)
- 1/2 teaspoon vanilla extract
- A pinch of salt
- 1/2 cup ice (optional, for a colder, thicker shake)
- Whipped cream and caramel sauce for garnish (optional)

Instructions:

1. **Prepare the Ingredients:**
   - If you're using store-bought crème caramel, make sure it's well-chilled before adding it to the shake. If you're using homemade crème caramel, ensure it's fully cooled.
2. **Blend Ingredients:**
   - In a blender, combine the crème caramel, vanilla ice cream, milk, caramel sauce, vanilla extract, and a pinch of salt.
   - Blend until smooth. If you like a thicker shake, add ice and blend again.
3. **Taste and Adjust:**
   - Taste the shake and adjust the sweetness or caramel flavor as needed. You can add more caramel sauce if you prefer a stronger caramel flavor.
4. **Serve:**
   - Pour the shake into glasses. For an extra touch, top with whipped cream and drizzle with additional caramel sauce.
5. **Enjoy:**
   - Serve immediately and enjoy the rich, creamy, and caramel-filled flavors!

This Crème Caramel Shake combines the smooth, luscious texture of crème caramel with the creamy goodness of ice cream, creating a decadent and delightful shake.

Fig and Honey Shake

Ingredients:

- 1 cup fresh or dried figs (if using dried, soak them in water for about 30 minutes to soften)
- 1 cup milk (or a dairy-free alternative like almond or oat milk)
- 1/2 cup Greek yogurt (plain or vanilla)
- 2 tablespoons honey (adjust to taste)
- 1/2 teaspoon vanilla extract
- 1/4 teaspoon ground cinnamon (optional, for added warmth)
- A pinch of salt
- 1/2 cup ice (optional, for a colder, thicker shake)
- Fresh figs or a drizzle of honey for garnish (optional)

Instructions:

1. **Prepare the Figs:**
   - If using dried figs, ensure they are softened by soaking them in water for about 30 minutes. Drain well before using. Fresh figs can be used directly after washing and removing stems.
2. **Blend Ingredients:**
   - In a blender, combine the figs, milk, Greek yogurt, honey, vanilla extract, ground cinnamon (if using), and a pinch of salt.
   - Blend until smooth. If you prefer a thicker consistency, add ice and blend again.
3. **Taste and Adjust:**
   - Taste the shake and adjust the sweetness or spice level as needed. Add more honey if you prefer it sweeter.
4. **Serve:**
   - Pour the shake into glasses. Garnish with fresh figs or a drizzle of honey if desired.
5. **Enjoy:**
   - Serve immediately and savor the sweet, creamy, and figgy goodness!

This Fig and Honey Shake is a wonderful way to enjoy the natural sweetness and unique flavor of figs combined with the richness of honey. It's perfect as a nutritious breakfast, a satisfying snack, or a light dessert.

Blueberry Lavender Shake

Ingredients:

- 1 cup fresh or frozen blueberries
- 1/2 cup Greek yogurt (plain or vanilla)
- 1/2 cup milk (or a dairy-free alternative like almond or oat milk)
- 1-2 tablespoons honey or maple syrup (adjust to taste)
- 1/2 teaspoon dried lavender buds (culinary grade)
- 1/2 teaspoon vanilla extract
- A pinch of salt
- 1/2 cup ice (optional, for a colder, thicker shake)
- Fresh blueberries or a sprig of lavender for garnish (optional)

Instructions:

1. **Infuse the Lavender:**
   - In a small bowl, mix the dried lavender buds with a little hot water (about 2 tablespoons) to steep for a few minutes. This helps release the flavor and fragrance. Strain out the lavender buds after steeping and let the lavender infusion cool slightly.
2. **Blend Ingredients:**
   - In a blender, combine the blueberries, Greek yogurt, milk, honey (or maple syrup), vanilla extract, a pinch of salt, and the cooled lavender infusion.
   - Blend until smooth. If you prefer a thicker shake, add ice and blend again.
3. **Taste and Adjust:**
   - Taste the shake and adjust the sweetness or lavender flavor if needed. Add more honey if you prefer it sweeter or a bit more lavender infusion if you want a stronger floral note.
4. **Serve:**
   - Pour the shake into glasses. Garnish with fresh blueberries or a sprig of lavender for an extra touch of elegance.
5. **Enjoy:**
   - Serve immediately and enjoy the blend of sweet blueberries with the delicate hint of lavender!

This Blueberry Lavender Shake is perfect for a refreshing summer drink, a unique brunch treat, or a sophisticated dessert. The combination of blueberry and lavender creates a beautifully balanced flavor that's both calming and delicious.

Vacherin Shake

Ingredients:

- 1/2 cup meringue cookies (store-bought or homemade, crumbled)
- 1 cup vanilla ice cream (or a dairy-free alternative)
- 1/2 cup milk (or a dairy-free alternative like almond or oat milk)
- 1/2 cup whipped cream (plus extra for topping)
- 1/2 cup fresh berries (e.g., raspberries, strawberries, or blueberries)
- 1-2 tablespoons honey or maple syrup (adjust to taste)
- 1/2 teaspoon vanilla extract
- A pinch of salt
- 1/2 cup ice (optional, for a colder, thicker shake)
- Fresh berries and additional meringue pieces for garnish (optional)

Instructions:

1. **Prepare the Meringue:**
   - If using store-bought meringue cookies, simply crumble them into small pieces. If making homemade meringues, let them cool completely before crumbling.
2. **Blend Ingredients:**
   - In a blender, combine the crumbled meringue cookies, vanilla ice cream, milk, whipped cream, fresh berries, honey (or maple syrup), vanilla extract, and a pinch of salt.
   - Blend until smooth. If you prefer a thicker shake, add ice and blend again.
3. **Taste and Adjust:**
   - Taste the shake and adjust the sweetness or berry flavor as needed. Add more honey if you prefer it sweeter or more berries if you like a stronger fruit flavor.
4. **Serve:**
   - Pour the shake into glasses. For a touch of elegance, top with extra whipped cream, fresh berries, and additional meringue pieces.
5. **Enjoy:**
   - Serve immediately and enjoy the delightful combination of creamy, fruity, and crispy textures!

This Vacherin Shake brings together the delightful flavors and textures of the classic dessert, offering a refreshing and satisfying treat that's perfect for any occasion.

Choco-Mint Macaron Shake

Ingredients:

- 2 chocolate macarons (store-bought or homemade, crumbled)
- 1 cup vanilla ice cream (or a dairy-free alternative)
- 1/2 cup milk (or a dairy-free alternative like almond or oat milk)
- 2 tablespoons chocolate syrup or melted dark chocolate
- 1/4 teaspoon peppermint extract (adjust to taste)
- 1/2 teaspoon vanilla extract
- A pinch of salt
- 1/2 cup ice (optional, for a colder, thicker shake)
- Whipped cream and extra macaron pieces or chocolate shavings for garnish (optional)

Instructions:

1. **Prepare the Macarons:**
   - If using store-bought macarons, crumble them into small pieces. If making homemade macarons, ensure they are fully cooled before crumbling.
2. **Blend Ingredients:**
   - In a blender, combine the crumbled macarons, vanilla ice cream, milk, chocolate syrup (or melted chocolate), peppermint extract, vanilla extract, and a pinch of salt.
   - Blend until smooth. If you prefer a thicker shake, add ice and blend again.
3. **Taste and Adjust:**
   - Taste the shake and adjust the sweetness or mint flavor as needed. Add more chocolate syrup if you want a richer chocolate flavor or a few more drops of peppermint extract if you like a stronger mint taste.
4. **Serve:**
   - Pour the shake into glasses. For an extra touch, top with whipped cream and garnish with additional macaron pieces or chocolate shavings.
5. **Enjoy:**
   - Serve immediately and savor the rich, creamy, and minty flavors!

This Choco-Mint Macaron Shake combines the decadent flavors of chocolate and mint with the elegant touch of macarons, making it a perfect treat for special occasions or just a luxurious dessert.

Blackberry Tart Shake

Ingredients:

- 1 cup fresh or frozen blackberries
- 1/2 cup vanilla ice cream (or a dairy-free alternative)
- 1/2 cup milk (or a dairy-free alternative like almond or oat milk)
- 1/4 cup graham cracker crumbs (for a tart-like base)
- 2 tablespoons honey or maple syrup (adjust to taste)
- 1/2 teaspoon vanilla extract
- A pinch of salt
- 1/2 cup ice (optional, for a colder, thicker shake)
- Whipped cream and additional graham cracker crumbs for garnish (optional)

Instructions:

1. **Prepare the Blackberries:**
    - If using fresh blackberries, wash them thoroughly. If using frozen, you can add them directly to the blender.
2. **Blend Ingredients:**
    - In a blender, combine the blackberries, vanilla ice cream, milk, graham cracker crumbs, honey (or maple syrup), vanilla extract, and a pinch of salt.
    - Blend until smooth. If you prefer a thicker shake, add ice and blend again.
3. **Taste and Adjust:**
    - Taste the shake and adjust the sweetness or tartness as needed. Add more honey if you prefer a sweeter shake or more graham cracker crumbs if you want a stronger tart-like flavor.
4. **Serve:**
    - Pour the shake into glasses. For an extra touch, top with whipped cream and sprinkle additional graham cracker crumbs on top.
5. **Enjoy:**
    - Serve immediately and enjoy the creamy, fruity, and tart flavors!

This Blackberry Tart Shake offers a deliciously creamy and fruity twist on the classic blackberry tart, making it a perfect treat for summer or any time you crave a refreshing, indulgent dessert.

Almond Cream Shake

Ingredients:

- 1/2 cup almonds (raw or roasted; if raw, soak them in water for a few hours or overnight)
- 1 cup vanilla ice cream (or a dairy-free alternative)
- 1/2 cup milk (or a dairy-free alternative like almond or oat milk)
- 1/4 cup almond cream or almond butter
- 2 tablespoons honey or maple syrup (adjust to taste)
- 1/2 teaspoon vanilla extract
- A pinch of salt
- 1/2 cup ice (optional, for a colder, thicker shake)
- Sliced almonds or a drizzle of almond butter for garnish (optional)

Instructions:

1. **Prepare the Almonds:**
   - If using raw almonds, soak them in water for a few hours or overnight to soften them. Drain and rinse them before use. If using roasted almonds, you can use them directly.
2. **Blend Ingredients:**
   - In a blender, combine the almonds, vanilla ice cream, milk, almond cream (or almond butter), honey (or maple syrup), vanilla extract, and a pinch of salt.
   - Blend until smooth. If you prefer a thicker shake, add ice and blend again.
3. **Taste and Adjust:**
   - Taste the shake and adjust the sweetness or almond flavor as needed. Add more honey if you prefer a sweeter shake or a bit more almond butter if you want a richer almond flavor.
4. **Serve:**
   - Pour the shake into glasses. For an extra touch, garnish with sliced almonds or a drizzle of almond butter.
5. **Enjoy:**
   - Serve immediately and enjoy the creamy, nutty, and indulgent flavors!

This Almond Cream Shake is perfect for those who love the rich, nutty flavor of almonds. It's smooth, creamy, and wonderfully satisfying, making it an ideal choice for a special treat.

Raspberry Chiffon Shake

Ingredients:

- 1 cup fresh or frozen raspberries
- 1/2 cup vanilla ice cream (or a dairy-free alternative)
- 1/2 cup milk (or a dairy-free alternative like almond or oat milk)
- 1/4 cup Greek yogurt (plain or vanilla, for a creamy texture)
- 2 tablespoons honey or maple syrup (adjust to taste)
- 1/2 teaspoon vanilla extract
- 1/4 teaspoon almond extract (optional, for added depth)
- A pinch of salt
- 1/2 cup ice (optional, for a colder, thicker shake)
- Whipped cream and fresh raspberries for garnish (optional)

Instructions:

1. **Prepare the Raspberries:**
   - If using fresh raspberries, wash them thoroughly. If using frozen raspberries, you can add them directly to the blender.
2. **Blend Ingredients:**
   - In a blender, combine the raspberries, vanilla ice cream, milk, Greek yogurt, honey (or maple syrup), vanilla extract, almond extract (if using), and a pinch of salt.
   - Blend until smooth. If you prefer a thicker shake, add ice and blend again.
3. **Taste and Adjust:**
   - Taste the shake and adjust the sweetness or flavor as needed. Add more honey if you prefer a sweeter shake or more raspberries if you want a stronger raspberry flavor.
4. **Serve:**
   - Pour the shake into glasses. For an extra touch, top with whipped cream and garnish with fresh raspberries.
5. **Enjoy:**
   - Serve immediately and savor the creamy, fruity, and elegant flavors!

This Raspberry Chiffon Shake offers a delightful combination of fresh raspberry flavor and creamy texture, with a touch of sophistication that makes it perfect for a special treat or a refreshing dessert.

Caramelized Banana Shake

Ingredients:

- 2 ripe bananas
- 2 tablespoons butter
- 3 tablespoons brown sugar
- 1 cup vanilla ice cream (or a dairy-free alternative)
- 1/2 cup milk (or a dairy-free alternative like almond or oat milk)
- 1/2 teaspoon vanilla extract
- A pinch of salt
- 1/2 cup ice (optional, for a colder, thicker shake)
- Whipped cream and additional caramel sauce for garnish (optional)

Instructions:

1. **Caramelize the Bananas:**
   - In a skillet over medium heat, melt the butter. Add the brown sugar and stir until it starts to dissolve and bubble.
   - Slice the bananas into rounds and add them to the skillet. Cook for 2-3 minutes on each side, or until the bananas are golden brown and caramelized. Remove from heat and let them cool slightly.
2. **Blend Ingredients:**
   - In a blender, combine the caramelized bananas, vanilla ice cream, milk, vanilla extract, and a pinch of salt.
   - Blend until smooth. If you prefer a thicker shake, add ice and blend again.
3. **Taste and Adjust:**
   - Taste the shake and adjust the sweetness or flavor if needed. You can add more honey or brown sugar if you want a sweeter shake.
4. **Serve:**
   - Pour the shake into glasses. For an extra touch of indulgence, top with whipped cream and drizzle with additional caramel sauce.
5. **Enjoy:**
   - Serve immediately and savor the rich, creamy, and caramelized banana flavors!

This Caramelized Banana Shake combines the caramelized richness of cooked bananas with the classic creamy texture of a milkshake, making it a decadent and satisfying treat.

Brioche Bread Pudding Shake

Ingredients:

- 2 cups brioche bread, cubed (about 2-3 slices)
- 1/2 cup milk (or a dairy-free alternative like almond or oat milk)
- 1/2 cup heavy cream (or a dairy-free alternative like coconut cream)
- 1/4 cup brown sugar
- 1 large egg
- 1/2 teaspoon vanilla extract
- 1/2 teaspoon ground cinnamon
- A pinch of salt
- 1 cup vanilla ice cream (or a dairy-free alternative)
- 1/2 cup ice (optional, for a colder, thicker shake)
- Whipped cream, caramel sauce, and a sprinkle of cinnamon for garnish (optional)

Instructions:

1. **Prepare the Bread Pudding:**
   - In a bowl, whisk together the milk, heavy cream, brown sugar, egg, vanilla extract, ground cinnamon, and a pinch of salt.
   - Add the cubed brioche bread to the mixture, ensuring that the bread is well soaked. Let it sit for about 10-15 minutes to absorb the liquid.
2. **Cook the Bread Pudding:**
   - Transfer the soaked bread mixture to a baking dish. Bake in a preheated oven at 350°F (175°C) for 25-30 minutes, or until the bread pudding is set and lightly browned on top. Allow it to cool slightly.
3. **Blend Ingredients:**
   - In a blender, combine the baked bread pudding, vanilla ice cream, and a pinch of salt. Blend until smooth. If you prefer a thicker shake, add ice and blend again.
4. **Taste and Adjust:**
   - Taste the shake and adjust the sweetness or spices if needed. You can add a bit more brown sugar or cinnamon if you like.
5. **Serve:**
   - Pour the shake into glasses. For an extra touch, top with whipped cream, a drizzle of caramel sauce, and a sprinkle of cinnamon.
6. **Enjoy:**
   - Serve immediately and enjoy the rich, creamy, and comforting flavors of this brioche bread pudding shake!

This Brioche Bread Pudding Shake offers a wonderful blend of buttery, sweet brioche with the creamy texture of a milkshake, making it a perfect indulgent treat for any time you want a dessert with a twist.

www.ingramcontent.com/pod-product-compliance
Lightning Source LLC
LaVergne TN
LVHW081325060526
838201LV00055B/2467